For Roland,
with thanks and all good wishes,

Norman Buller

Powder on the Wind

First published in 2011
by Waterloo Press (Hove)
95 Wick Hall
Furze Hill
Hove BN3 1NG

Printed in Palatino by
One Digital
54 Hollingdean Road
East Sussex BN2 4AA

© Norman Buller 2011

All rights remain with the author.

Cover design © Waterloo Design 2011
Cover photo © treatment of a photo by Matilda Persson 2011

Norman Buller is hereby identified as author of this work in accordance with Section 77 of the Copyright, Designs and Patents Act 1988

This book is sold subject to the condition that it shall not, by way of trade or otherwise, be lent, resold, hired out or otherwise circulated without the author's prior consent in any form of binding or cover other than that in which it is published and without a similar condition including this condition being imposed on the subsequent purchaser.

A CIP record for this book is available from the British Library

ISBN 978-1-906742-34-8

Acknowledgements

Thanks are due to the editors of the following publications in which some of my work has previously appeared. These include:

Acumen; Agenda; California Quarterly (USA); *The Comstock Review* (USA); *Communique* (South Africa); *Envoi; Gravesiana; The Interpreter's House; Iota; The London Magazine; Orbis; Other Poetry; Outposts; Poetry from Cambridge; Poetry Life; Poetry News; Poetry Nottingham; Poetry Salzburg Review* (Austria); *The Rialto*.

My work has also been awarded prizes in *Poetry Life*, Bedford Poetry and Ware Poetry competitions.

By the same author

Fools and Mirrors (Waterloo Press, 2010)
Sleeping With Icons (Waterloo Press, 2007)
Travelling Light (Waterloo Press, 2005)
Thirteen Poems (Festival Publications,
	Queen's University Belfast, 1965)

Contents

Part I

William Langland	1
The Ravens	2
Eager Tomb	3
Aleksandr Blok	4
Girl with Two Dogs	6
Sickert's London	7
The Purpose of a Zoo	8
The Waldstein Sonata	9
Louis MacNeice	10
Daybreak in Prague	11
From a Japanese Garden	12
Strasbourg in August	13
The Flesh Made Word	14
Man of My Time	15
Powder on the Wind	16

What The Preacher Said I

Psalm	19
Beyond the Visible	20
Going Forth by Day	21
Stumbling at Noon	22
The Wisdom of Tao-Te Ching	23
Kabbalah	24
Veda	25
Zarathushtra	26
Song of the Lord	27
Through the Gates	28

Part II

At the Grave of Wystan Auden	31
Ignorant Desire	33
Café in the Place Pigalle	34
Siberian Crossing	35
Romantics	36
Osip Mandelshtam	37
Dream of Fair Woman	38
A Professor Asleep	39
Othello	40
Elizabeth Bishop Comes to Tea	41
Autumn Song	42
Where's Love?	43
Robert Graves, *Poeta*	44
Ancient Winter	46
A Husband Visits the Cancer Ward	47
Otherness	48
Marina Tsvetayeva	49
Odalisque with Red Trousers	51
Leda in Byzantium	52
Utrillo in Montmartre	53

What The Preacher Said II

All Are Dust	57
Autumn Leaves	58
Working for the Wind	59
Shiva's Hair	60
Song for the Dead	61
Egyptian Sunrise	62
A Cry in the Street	63
Revelation	64
The Path	65
Days of Darkness	66

Part III

Isaac Rosenberg	69
Crocuses	70
Monet's Impression: sunrise	71
Loïe Fuller at the Folies Bergère	72
Hospital Visit	73
Prince Pasternak	74
Obsession	75
Apocalypse	76
Third Symphony in White	77
Nobody's	78
Another Morning	79
Tchaikovski's Mistress	80
Gwen John	81
At the Auschwitz Factory	82
The Poet to His Soul	83

To
Fircroft College, Birmingham
and
St. Catharine's College, Cambridge
in lasting gratitude

Let not the thread of my song
Be cut while I sing
And let not my work end
Before its fulfilment

The Rig Veda

Part I

William Langland

Let it be daybreak
on Malvern hillsides
with gorse garlands
in gayest yellow
and waking creatures
lovingly cradled
in morning's opening hand.

Then let us dare
in deliberate dream
to summon again
those semblant sights,
the scenes of faerie,
with friars at fairs
fooling with promise of pardon.

Better to measure
the mist on a local
hillside than listen
to unctuous usurers
mouthing their mean
religion of money
in the field full of folk.

Long, lean Will
of the Hills, now wander
once more among us
in fitting form
to flay our shallow
and shameful greed;
still sing of the saving of souls.

The Ravens
after Arthur Rimbaud

Lord, when the meadows have grown cold
in lonely hamlets left to rot
and the sad evening bells have shot
their bolt, let ravens make their bold
assault on nature in demise,
swooping from vast, aggressive skies.

Battalions of raucous sounds,
may your nests soon disintegrate
in icy winds. You'll relocate
after dispersal, do the rounds
of holes and ditches, then liaise
with yellow streams and Calvary ways.

Flock in your masses above lands
of France where thousands of war dead
lie in their graves; become a dread
reminder, whirling in vast bands
above, to forgetful passers-by,
black omens in a funereal sky.

You saints of heaven in the oak,
that ruined mast of evening's charm,
do not do summer songbirds harm;
let them, for those below, invoke
an anthem for that last retreat
and mark their futureless defeat.

Eager Tomb

Prime for death's curfew,
our secret atrocities
already gather.
Our history shadows us
like an eager tomb, our grave
already dug but unseen.

The forbidding hill,
on waking, is always there.
Each day ends; I'm still
this side of it. Night forgets;
I wake, there it is, waiting
to be climbed, day after day.

We hoard somewhere the
bilge and molten gold of our
experience. So,
when we cease, what can it do
but ebb to source, like water
to water where ripples fade?

Aleksandr Blok
(1880 – 1921)

She's always there. I keep
her fire lit.   Certainly
I serve her.   Even asleep
she still amazes me.

I'm just a fish, fast-hooked;
played out, reeled back for more.
My hellish goose is cooked
by this half-saint, half whore.

From church comes the slow moan
of Mass.   Heart, stifle all
your hymns.   Know to the bone
life's an unanswered call.

What's happiness?   A lazy
doze after meals.   But then
you wake and the whole crazy
circus starts up again.

We're only here to lose
life's game; it's how we are.
I keep hitting the booze
that screws me to the bar.

My fantasies go back
to darkness, dirt and stink —
humiliation's track.
Christ, how I need that drink!

Russia, worse hell's ahead.
Prise open your fate's lips
and hear it groan, with dread,
your doom's apocalypse.

I've testified, lip curled
in scorn.   It's time to go.
I hate life, loathe the world,
shout at the present — 'NO!'

Girl with Two Dogs

The dog caressed
within her heart
is nothing like
in any part
the animal who pads around
sniffing his mistress' spoor
along the ground.

The dog inside
has fiery eye
fierce claws that rip
and teeth that try
to tear affection and contest
to breach the bone-cage prison
of her breast.

The dog outside
remains unwise
begging her with
his craven eyes
to break that fascination in
the beast she fondles deep
so deep within.

Sickert's London

Losing his virginity
at fourteen to a milkmaid,
he flirted briefly
with the Victorian stage,
next paying court
to Whistler's butterfly,
learning the art
of acting through the paint.

Afterwards the sawdust and spittoons,
enclosed, stuffy interiors,
models in dingy rooms
and dust on mirrors,
whores on iron beds,
brooding Islington and Camden Town —
Jack Ripper's parish —
and Crippen's Finsbury Park.

The deaf canvas listened;
in texture that could
strike a match
he figured life
at an unguarded moment
through features, gesture, pose
in publicans and sinners,
claustrophobic marriages

in enigmatic rooms,
erotic melancholy
in the shadows,
haunting the gloomy
empty squares in winter,
lurking about the
furtive dark and light,
painting the silence.

The Purpose of a Zoo

Which is the basest creature, man or beast?
Birds feed on birds, beasts on each other prey
But savage man alone does man betray
          John Wilmot, Earl of Rochester

They do not volunteer;
the animals are there,
angry, patiently watchful,
or broken in despair,
captive for shallow curiosity
or crass amusement.

Wild beasts
do not demean themselves,
as we do,
with their own bondage.

Could it be that
the purpose of a zoo
is to acquaint us all
with our enslavement,
just as the barbed-wire fence
informs the guard
that he, too, is a prisoner?

The Waldstein Sonata

Solitary ballerina
pointing with exciting grace,
turns to nimbly playing hopscotch
deftly square to square.

Pensive now in gentle movement
on and off a throbbing drum,
wondering if someone's watching,
hoping she is loved.

Vibrant, like a rage imprisoned
in a cat's cradle of sound;
it escapes between the lattice,
courts and lays the ear.

Ludwig's new Erard piano
spins his matrix of near-song,
lures our fantasy which enters
naïve as a fly.

Louis MacNeice

When he was five the black dreams came,
dragging him from his private dark,
no angel at his door.   Waking
brought only desolate day. He walked
with no more choice than a falling stone,
a nomad who had lost his tent,
murmuring prayers all gods would shun.
Come back early or never come.

His mother deserted him for the misty
boatman who rowed her over his river,
left him a mythic land of broken
statues and passing trains puffing
their epitaphs of smoke in silent
terror across the sky.   By day
his father seemed a chilly sun.
Come back early or never come.

Dandy and rebel, his Oxford was Classics,
windows and mirrors, an unlit lamp,
a garden planted with paper flowers.
She came again to his unshared nights
though only an episode, leaving him
as the boy in Aeschylus chasing a bird
in a dark wood, the straight way gone.
Come back early or never come.

In his life it was always autumn;
whatever happened, the Quest went on.
The middle years are bad for a poet
lamenting the maker he might have become.
But — down the hatch! Light another one! —
as she played locked heart and the lost key
endlessly on her sickening drum.
Come back early or never come.

[10]

Daybreak in Prague
after Nazim Hikmet

In Prague it's slowly getting light
and now snow falls,
sleety and grey.

The first tram rumbles out;
its windows warmly glow
and yet inside it is still icy-cold.

Baroque façades, aloof and ill-at-ease,
slowly grow light,
their gilt black with grief.

The statues on Charles Bridge
seem like birds
fallen from lifeless stars.

I drive a horse-drawn wagon
past the Old Jewish Cemetery
and pine for another city.

Inside the Cemetery
death is still as stones
and does not breathe.

My rose!
My absent rose!
Exile is worse than death.

From a Japanese Garden

Blossom of a tree
in light breeze gently brushing
the face: a courtship.

Shadows of the trees
tremble on the lawn, then fade,
stressing your absence.

In age all blossoms
shed their petals except the
blooms of memory.

When you are silent
I am satisfied because
you do not say no.

My verse seeks beauty
deep in the heart's unfathomed
murmuring waters.

I offer you my
verses, inarticulate
tokens of sorrow.

Tangled life, shall I
ever learn how to smoothly
weave your wayward strands?

Strasbourg in August

The Cathedral withers now,
flowering only
in its sacred past

as moneychangers and tourists
crawl like aphids
over its body.

Buskers and clowns
make a fairground
at its door.

The sky darkens;
ancient, delicate houses
preen before visitors

as the town
fattens its wallet
and a drunken woman

gropes for the carousel,
stumbles and sprawls
in the rain.

The Flesh Made Word

I thought at first she'd come
to raise my pulse and wake
my body into heat.
It wasn't so.

Then that I would succumb
to fleshless love and take
pleasure in that defeat.
That was not so.

At last, seeking her dumb
intent, and for the sake
of having her complete,
wanting it so,

I saw these words become
her purpose, saw she'd make
me know her by this feat,
but only so.

Man of My Time
after Salvatore Quasimodo

Even now you carry a sling and stone,
man of my time.   You sat in hatred's cockpit,
winged and ready, instruments set for death
— I saw you!   You were in the armoured car,
you manned the gallows and the torturer's wheel
— yes, I saw it!   It was you all right,
you and your careful science of destruction,
loveless and without Christ.   Today you kill
as you always did, as your ancestors always killed.

Your stench of blood is as foul, man of my time,
as when that murderer said to his brother,
"Let us go to the fields".   Its chilling echo
is still sounding deep within you, in
the very bones of your life.   Blast from your
memory the vapours of blood that rise
and swirl from the earth.   Blot out your ancestors;
force the wind to shatter their tombs to dust
and let the birds' black wings fold over their hearts.

Powder on the Wind

Each day's end
tells of our finite span
squandered on passing things,
pounding each other's lives
to dust on air.

We have lost nature's ear,
no longer nurture days
as we would garner
transient harvest
to fend off winter.

Once our lives turned
with the year's wheel;
the seasons saw
we never broke
our bond with earth.

Now we're frittered away
on the sheen of things,
ground in the ceaseless
mill of gold
to powder on the wind.

What The Preacher Said

I

As all men are alike (tho' infinitely various), So all Religions

William Blake

Psalm

The sky is my father,
the earth my bountiful mother.
I walk in the dark
but seek the footprints of gods.

Free me from anger
and lure of wine and dice.
Cast my transgressions away
like loosening bonds.

I ask my own heart
'When shall I find the Eternal?'
I ask the god in all things
to cherish my songs.

Beyond the Visible

Who can see
beyond the visible world?
Did we have life
before the world began?

Look around us.
We are living
but do not know true life.
The world does not know us;
we do not know ourselves.

There will be fire,
then darkness will cover the earth.
There will be no light
from sun, moon or stars.

Each of us
is the indweller of all beings.
We are what we believe.
All streams run to the sea.

Going Forth by Day

I am the master of limits;
I rise from the egg
in the hidden land.

I come in the form of sunrise
from the water
of the river of forgetting.

I am the singer
unbolting the door
of hidden light.

Wisdom is hidden
in the essence of all,
in the seeds of eternity.

I have split heaven
and passed through the horizon
on my way to wisdom.

Stumbling at Noon

Transgressors from the womb,
we're silent in the dust;
joy in the land has gone.

We are as greedy dogs
who never have enough,
each of us for his gain.

We're like the troubled sea
whenever it can't rest,
casting up dirt and mire.

We stumble at broad noon,
groping for the wall
as if we had no eyes.

Truth's fallen in the street.
We droop like shrivelled leaves
for we are as the dead.

The Wisdom of Tao-Te Ching

Fish cannot abandon water;
live where the greatest treasure is Charity
or suffer the thorns of emptiness.

Should the Great Way be cast aside,
much must be hard
like treading on melting ice.

Return to the root,
the root of Light,
and grasp ancient ways.

Days stubbornly endure.
Fix on lacking desire;
sages desire not to desire.

What is not guided ends quickly.
Those who tiptoe may never arrive
and a long walk starts with one footstep.

Kabbalah

Lightning spears out of heaven
in the battle against chaos.

'Woe to whoever closes the gate'
thunder the gods.

Strew your dead on the fields
to nourish your crops.

The wilderness must bloom again,
the deaf must hear, the dumb sing
and the lame run like the stag.

The eye of the Infinite does not sleep.
His voice spreads glory upon the waters
and see — light at sunrise!

Veda

In the beginning
dark was hidden by dark;
no night or day,
no death or immortality.

Then came an impulse beneath
and a giving forth above
and Creation happened,
bringing sacrifice and flesh-eating fire.

Verses and chants were born
and from them poetry;
let the songs of poets
waft you to endless time.

The All-Maker is vast
in mind and strength
but many will not find him
because the god of ignorance

has come between them
with false priests glutted
with earthly pleasure
and minds puffy with cloud.

Zarathushtra

Search for the truth of the Wise Lord,
the origin of light and darkness
far beyond the path of the sun.

Search for the Wise Lord's holy goblet
by the glittering thoughts of the stars
and the sacred utterance of the moon.

To reach the kingdom yet to come,
scorn all followers of the Lie
doomed to expire in the circle of vultures,

caught in the arms of the hideous hag
who will dip them into the River of Fire
and try their souls on the fourth day.

Death will free your soul from bondage;
then it may cross the bridge of dogs
to be embraced by the maidens of heaven.

All this is written in holy books:
the sacred fire must burn for ever.
Thus spoke Zarathushtra.

Song of the Lord

Lord of the Winds, how shall I ever know you?

Only by conquering self, the lusts of 'I',
those puppets in a play of shadows. Know
I am the quench in water, brightness in flame,
scents of the earth, the seed of all our being,
the mood and impulse of the wandering moon.

Know that you are alive in every being
as every being lives in you. Who works
with love for all creation works with me.
These words are pearls strung on the Infinite.
One is the source of All — that is my truth.

Lord of the Winds, how shall I ever know you?

Through the Gates

Why did the Golden City cease?
Fear had petrified our hearts
and justice lay beyond our reach.

Now the deceived heart
has turned aside
and feeds on ashes.

My tongue is a sharpened blade;
when the bough withers
it shall be cut off.

On the day the towers fall
we shall stretch ourselves and rise
from the stones of emptiness.

Enter — go now through the gates;
make the wilderness like Eden
and the desert blossom like the rose.

Part II

At the Grave of Wystan Auden

As I, one of the many lives
you never perceived, stand aware
of you this May morning, beneath
their stolid headstones and arabesqued
ironwork of your Martyr's cross,
the Kirchstetten dead, even the Nazi
suicide long-levelled in his
separate garden, are imperceptibly
crumbling back into their village
as earth to earth.   Always a fugitive
hunted by soldiers while love hid
beyond the uncrossable border, you shuddered,
unready, into an early fame;
now, in your country of unconcern,
is the bruise of your youth still as blue?

Innocence came to its sudden end;
deep in your lead-mined limestone landscape
with thwarting passages, hollowed caverns,
the echoing trickle of hidden water
secret and fickle as mankind,
you and your brothers, rival lovers,
explored your mother's forbidding slopes,
that awesome mythic being you
could never imagine copulating.
How to break out? How to be whole?
You sang Isolde to her Tristan
but when she died the music stopped;
you were alone; in that cold void
you reached for Christ, a door through which,
at last, the Answer glowed like fire.

But limestone cannot bond in love
and when, in human guise, it crossed
your frontier you were still denied.
Then, in the night of fire and snow,
infidelity tolled like a murderous
bell summoning the hurt to kill,
dooming you to the loneliness
of any mirror into which
no-one is gazing. Because you, too,
have long entered another kind
of wood, I stand at a simple door
into the earth that closed forever
on an anguished man. All you made
can be held here this one moment
and does not burn the hand.

Ignorant Desire

Your green-banked river
forms again and flows.
I water at a hole
where no grass grows

and in that thirsting
fever grope your land
only to find parched bones
in dust and sand.

You have a self
my needless self could know,
but through my ignorant
desire you go

a mere ghost of possession.
Which is true?
Need of your body
disembodies you.

Café in the Place Pigalle

It's welcome to the theatre,
black coffee and a glass of booze,
Desboutin's bowler on the tilt
and Ellen's bunchy hat and shoes.

It's welcome to the studio too,
the models costumed for their parts
and Degas, pitiless, at work
with French and oriental arts.

All this is serious. Here, with care,
players and props are set in place
that moment before tears could fill
the joyless chasm in her face

for Paris favours only few.
Their two blurred shadows widen; they
sit trapped in Degas' loneliness
at tables in the sad café.

Siberian Crossing
after Evgeny Vinokurov

The restaurant car's designer promised comfort
throughout a thousand miles. Strangers together,
they share a bottle, sing or mildly argue,
and tear each others' already-wounded hearts.

That sailor's going back to base from leave;
this bushy-eyebrowed actor starts a tour;
for endless miles they sit together, feeling
a temporary, artificial sameness

against their wills. Knowing it cannot last,
each fumbles for the pain of half a lifetime
and spreads it out before each open heart
where secrets slip their bonds without a cost.

A hidden life, failed marriage, separation,
shameful betrayal — all crawl from dark to daylight;
the need in human nature for confession
proves stronger than reserve! How many poems,

stories or novels are heaped here? How could one
possibly not go mad trying to cram them
all into the pockets of one's memory?
The passengers ride on and mumble back

to diffidence. Light follows dark, then light
again, then dark, breaking over their faces.
How they long to forget! Outside their windows
Siberia's forests stretch for a thousand miles.

Romantics

Sometimes, in the dark hours,
she comes to me again
just as she was
though now bearing no albatross,
the corpse of her marriage tossed
into some ditch.

While others languished in the everyday,
we'd climb Italian cliffs with Adonais,
Childe Harold and Endymion.   She'd said
"You spent your last pence on a book of verse!
How wise, wiser than you may ever know."
Then, wistfully, "I too caught on the air
the heady fume of art
but let it waft away on a passing wind.
I've lived a life of dross.
You are still young;
promise me you'll ignore the commonplace —
and never betray your spark."

I long to ask each time how she can bear
to crawl once more over the rubbish tip
of our two wasteland pasts,
to drag herself again over that rancid
landfill of putrified desires,
corrupted hopes, dead dreams?
But, as I try to speak,
she places finger to lip
and fades before the dawn.

Osip Mandelshtam
(1891-1938)

My country shudders through an evil time.
A black sun breeds its tumour in our days.
The Kremlin Master savours murders; I'm
rolled on his tongue like a berry. Our motherland prays

then sleeps in her coffin. The air hangs thick and heavy
with the stench of fear. The bedrock seeths with worms.
We are wandering through a crowded cemetery
without faith in resurrection, which confirms

that the wax of our mortality melts fast.
We burn like candles at noon, though not for long.
But where heart's truth picks the lock of silence at last,
when all has vanished there'll be space, the stars, the song.

Dream of Fair Woman

Man has dreamed his legend
of fair woman
centuries long:

gentle, fragile, submissive
keeper of the feminine
flame, adored

by troubadours in song
and waiting for
a passing knight

to pause, Grail-driven,
bent on courtesy,
thrall to her beauty.

But, at the ultimate tryst,
the dream fails
and there she stands

in armour, plume aloft,
visor down,
sword loosened,
her gauntlet flung at his feet.

A Professor Asleep

There's such a lot of mechanical engineering
in that old brainbox, rusted and fatigued
all of it, even the endless peering
from habit into learned publications.

Articles by young contemporaries
no longer quicken his thought or even rouse
nostalgic hopes or envious memories;
just so many fingerholds up the glacier

of professional fortune to where he sits already,
crumpled and mouth agape, his reputation
thinning against the wind, asleep.
And yet he clears our pity;

stirring, the fog of gears
about his head thins and parts in his dreams
and the lost sun, breaking through junkyard fears,
flashes on fishing rods and old Welsh streams.

Othello

Skins,
dark or fair:
thin veneers which peel
in marriage beds.

Not in patrician Venice!
There it's dyed in the wool,
festers the General's soul,
welcomes the poison in his ear,
corrupts his armour.

Led by the nose,
career is hurled aside,
his name blackens like skin
and honesty's a word,
a toy in the mouth,
a lamp across a swamp;
trust it — and drown!

Elizabeth Bishop Comes to Tea

The wandering lady reaches my gate
but hesitates
as if not sure she ought to be there,
then contemplates

the thinning cloud of her mission, hoping
for positive sign
that the house she's supposed to arrive at
should really be mine.

My door stands open.   She enters and sits
on a vacant settee,
spreads her dress widely round her and asks
"Is it time now for tea?"

Nothing to eat but her pilgrim heart
as it sorrowed and bled,
nothing to drink but her hundred poems
which I hadn't read.

"The sad seamstress said I should come,
that I just might belong.
But then, she was always so hopeless and bitter
— and always so wrong!"

Autumn Song
after the troubadour Cercamon

As bitter autumn wind
tears at the ailing leaves,
look on me here and find
a prisoner who grieves
always for my love's heart
though she may never part

with it, and I am worn
with waiting. Torn by care,
I am one who was born
to fill the trap and snare
of love. Yet I enjoy
the pain which could destroy

me for, being her gift, even
pain is beautiful.
Though through this hell-in-heaven
her heart stays ever cruel,
he is no true courtier
to whom love brings despair.

Where's Love?

Suppose our souls incline
to worlds beyond this place;
there love will play by different
rules from ours.

No space or time confine
the spirit's pure embrace;
our disembodiment
extends love's powers.

But here I'm no Dante
nor you a Beatrice,
the female he could love
void in the air.

Here soul and spirit play
the roles our bodies fix.
Where's love, unless you prove
tangibly there?

Robert Graves, *Poeta*

Fearing his awesome mother,
the trenches' cruelty
and neurasthenic terror
copied his inner war.
He galloped his marriage-bed
with Materfamilias,
booted and cruelly spurred,
astride his back.

He worshipped a Great Mistress
who guaranteed his art;
she came from another country
preaching unholy writ,
the guardian of a secret
wisdom which he could suffer
only through her; there at her
crumbling feet he grovelled
for his pain.

Under a phallic hammer
his Idol broke, so lost
her esoteric power.
A gentler woman came
with no ordeals or torments,
no sorcery but only
uncomplicated love;
their peace and tenderness
thawed out each other's winter
in a bleak Devon.

But in his mental womb
a creature was conceived
then born — the White Goddess,
a mythic metaphor
of purity and terror.
He'd stared into the heart
of love and dreamed it barren.
Come, mighty Mother, Muse
and Mistress, mount his flanks
again; he craves your spur
to goad reluctant art
from misery!

Time would wear out his body,
whiten his hair but bring
no wisdom; the surgeon's knife
would hasten drooling-time.
Then he would relive
those wild white women of
Euripides in the groves
of Dei, pitiless furies
come to torment his age,
chasing those Jill-O-Lanterns
over their perilous mires
into oblivion.

Ancient Winter
after Salvatore Quasimodo

Your hands, desirable, glowed white
in the dark aura of the flame;
they had the fragrance and delight
of oak and roses.   Winter came

with death and hungry birds.   Then snow
covered them suddenly.   Quick!   Bring
fragments of sun, angel's halo
and just ourselves in ethereal morning.

A Husband Visits the Cancer Ward

Each time they inject
it is his needle
entering the moist portals
of her disease;
the muffling of pain
is his discharge,
his ecstasy of numbing.

Love without hope
drifts powerless
in the scrubbed air
where oblivion circles,
patient for carrion.
It's time to leave again,
the white coats closing in.

Otherness

How separate you are,
newly born,
spasmed at last from the womb,
bloodied and new;
the cold, your trauma,
the shocked breath you draw,
bellow your utter selfhood
to the world.

How separate you are,
closest love;
no one-ness we, only
our differing selves
make love possible;
only when you are most
completely you can I
entirely love you.

How separate you are,
one who died,
even more other-than-me
as a corpse than when
alight with life;
more absent than a snuffed
flame, the candle living
to burn again.

Marina Tsvetayeva
(1892-1941)

You, my final night —
friend or enemy — dine
well on my sorrow, despite
my poems stored like wine.

You tell me it's over, calling
out through storms and calms
that I'm a harlot sprawling
in a drunken Russia's arms.

But no-one lays a finger
on me; haughty and poor,
I am both song and singer
and the beggar at your door.

You read me with dismay?
Don't ask me what I mean;
what do rivers say
to the banks they flow between?

I always felt a gypsy
urge to move on, heading west,
so don't light a candle for me;
graveyard strawberries are best.

Life's been a message in code;
I can't get the hang of it.
This rope I hold is a road
that leads me straight to the pit.

It seems I have no choice;
nightmares won't let me waken.
Once I'd been given a voice
everything else was taken.

[49]

In death's flux, I dare say,
I'll lose this pain, these scars.
May what was yesterday
waist-high soon touch the stars.

Odalisque with Red Trousers
after Henri Matisse

I am not here;
what you see is
a form among forms
setting curves
against straight lines,
defining space
in terms of colour.

Here I am only
a door which lets him
enter a garden
where he can be
alone and happy
not portraying a woman
but making a picture.

Yet I had to come
to him many times
before he'd finished with me.
Was I a spatial problem
he had to solve
or something buried
too deep to understand?

Leda in Byzantium

Yeats' shudder in the loins is natural drive,
requires no god as swan.   Sex walks with death.
The apple's bitten because we're alive,
set in equation with our final breath.

Out of the womb we start to wear away;
each breath will move us nearer to our dying
as well as to our making life.   Today
the shudder, then tomorrow's infant crying.

The cycle holds us; we turn on its spit
from nappies on to school, wet dreams or bras,
then work and parenthood — survival kit
for merely growing old, grandpas, grandmas.

Youth's landscape has no lake for age to swim in.
That is no country for old men — or women!

Utrillo in Montmartre

Speedily, impatiently
refashioning his soul
in a painted world
where humans are baubles
and only houses and cafés
have personality,

he rose again,
day after day,
on the hill of martyrs
where trees' skeletal hands
groped the sky and
eyeless sockets of flats

dotted his landscape,
where broad-haunched
women he loathed
were forever strutting
away from him;
this new martyr, beaten,

crucified on the bottle
and beaten again,
set on the featureless
masks of his skies
his wordless story;
in alcohol the colours flowed.

What The Preacher Said

II

As all men are alike (tho' infinitely various), So all Religions

William Blake

All Are Dust

Everything has time and season
but man does not truly know his time.

I came into this world with vanity
but must I depart in darkness?

I gave my heart to know wisdom
but in darkness could not find it.

Must what happens to the fool
happen to me?

Let there be hope for the living
though all is vanity

for all are dust.

Autumn Leaves

There should be neither poverty nor riches
but the rich are lords of the poor,
the borrower beholden to the lender.

Rather than wealth, treasure a good name.
Those who worship riches lack understanding,
scorning the poor begging at their gate.

When will the wealthy waken?
They too will cry in turn, hoping to be heard,
when wealth from greed falls like autumn leaves.

Working for the Wind

I look at all my labour
and see no profit;
there is no gain
in working for the wind.

The race is not to the swift
nor the battle to the strong.
Where is wisdom or justice
in the tomb?

Consider all oppression,
the tears that have no comforter.
Wisdom nurtures whoever follows it
but who can find what is distant and deep?

Sorrows haunt our days
but hatred and envy perish in the grave
and what is now shall be forgotten
in days to come.

Shiva's Hair

Sing of a goddess flowing
from a most holy place
like a celestial river
over the sky's face

who would have drowned the earth
had she not tangled there
magically netted
in Shiva's matted hair

and, there reprieved, descended
to flow wild to the sea
within wide banks confining
her wayward liberty,

singing the god of destruction
who, sleeping now, will soon
come riding on a burning ram
lit by a blazing moon.

Song for the Dead

Go away, Death,
go by a path of your own,
not by a path of the gods.
Dead one, I heap

the earth around you;
on a day yet to come
I too will be lain in earth
as you lie now.

Return with longing
to lords of sacred speech,
to the ancient ones;
adore them with your songs.

Egyptian Sunrise

Sun and moon
are eyes of the Eternal.
I cry in the absence of the moon.

I am the lion
striding from the pool
of double fire.

In the time before sunrise
I sever the head
of the snake of darkness.

I come from the flames
in the rising
eye of the sun.

A Cry in the Street

Wisdom shouts into the wind;
when destruction threatens
listen to her cry.

Wisdom cries in the street;
scorn her at your peril
for the way of a fool thinks folly wise.

Wisdom has built her house of seven pillars
to stand against the hurricane
but the fool waits houseless beyond the gates.

Revelation

A figure stood there all in white,
his eyes glowing with golden fire;
in his right hand he held seven stars.

I am the first and the last, he said.
I can show you an open door
which no-one can ever close.

I stood at the open door; beheld
a pale horse whose rider was Death
with Hell on pillion, grief for mankind.

I saw seven lamps burning in darkness
and a book bearing seven seals
while seven thunders uttered their voices.

Then a great mountain, lit with fire,
fell to the sea and the sea was blood
and many people died in the waters.

I heard an angel who stood in the sun
say: 'Destroy those who destroy the earth
and I will bring you the morning star.'

The Path

I sing of the immortal journey
of creation scattered over the world,
of rain sent from the drenching sky
to quicken the dead earth.

You are a raindrop in the ocean,
a grain of sand on the beach of the world,
a spec of dust in the shifting wind;
walk in humility.

I sing of created male and female,
union of lover and beloved.
Plant your tree and nurture it
in the orchard of Truth.

Cross the bridge sharper than a sword
and thinner than a single hair;
follow the caravan of Love
wherever its camels turn.

Days of Darkness

In the words of the preacher,
rise at the voice of the bird
and the daughters of music.

Cast your bread upon the waters
and it will return in kind.
All that was written is upright
and the making of books will endure.

Live many years in rejoicing
but remember the days of darkness
for they shall be many.
Walk in ways of the heart
and behold the sun.

Part III

Isaac Rosenberg

His twin born dead, he sought a missing
part of himself; broke free, became
the Slade School solitary, wearing
poverty as his albatross.
The matrons who paid his fees were hurt
that he wouldn't fawn, cut him adrift.
No matter!   He would bruise the air
with words jabbing like clenched fists.

His Jewish momma wore the breeches,
his benefactors held the purse;
women were power, the serpent in
the kiss, ruin within their hair,
dangerous tides in which to quench
his thighs' fire.   His thought's worm
stiffened to the fear.   How fiercely his
adversity burned for an iron death!

It was someone else's war.   The whims
of murder were oddly stable, a human
landscape deeper and wider than
the spattered brains and crunched bone.
It was lice hunting, poppies and rats
and dawn birdsong, letters and sneers,
blasphemy, mud and sex, the blade
thrust in and out, breeding and killing.

Crocuses

Amid the decadence
of how we live
the crocuses emerge,
oblivious to everything
that isn't nature.

How the thrust
of their small, simple lives
pushes them into blossom!
How we look in wonder
at their mindless dedication,

seeing what persists
against the tide!   Their presence
reminds us of what dies
and must renew
despite the odds.

Monet's Impression: sunrise

Light nears
granting the eye
the gift visible

as boatmen furthest
from the sun
oar in the dark

and upper
clouds flush
at the sun's touch

while furled
ships form
grey as ghosts

and the sea
bleeds under
the sun's knife.

Loïe Fuller at the Folies Bergère
after Toulouse-Lautrec

A dance on fire,
the blue and green turning
in the swirl of lit silk
and the silk burning

about her body,
snaking in seaweed curl
curving upward.   There
in billow and whirl

to the tip of her hidden
hand the arabesque flows
where, in the Dance of the Lilies,
a lily grows.

Hospital Visit

Death is a sure thing,
whether we're soon to die
or only visiting.

Should we savour delay
as thrilling progress, cling
like hell to life's decay?

Maybe we plunder time
like petty thieves, each day
only a minor crime

we get away with — that's,
till the last!   The lime
pit waits; till then my hat's

still in the shrinking ring
and, though we trek salt-flats,
my cup dips in your spring.

Prince Pasternak
(1890-1960)

I'm at the footlights, listening for echoes,
hearing the future rage, its belly full
of disaster. Death is now on stage and goes
between the gravestones, staring at my skull.

Yes, I would act the part, although I felt
the play was hardly mine. A blend of ink
and sobbing formed the bitter words that spelt
my truer role. Father, I'm at the brink.

Take my life from the shelf and blow its dust
away; what is foretold will be revealed.
I'll make the blank page flower if I must;
life's not a lazy jaunt across a field!

Obsession
after Charles Baudelaire

Enormous woods, you terrify me like
cathedrals with your organ roar. In our
defiled hearts' funereal chambers strike
your echoing chords, hour by endless hour.

Ocean, I hate you. In your crazed distress
I hear my mind's tumult. The malady
of man's defeated snigger of duress
sobs in the massive laughter of the sea.

Night, please me — rid yourself of stars, for their
glow speaks a language I well understand.
I crave the bleak and bare, not this ghost-land
where shadows portray thousands whose eyes stare

back into mine, lost beings I recognize,
haunting my past with vengeance in their eyes.

Apocalypse

Brute Nature craves
that life should flow
from him to her,
indifferent
whether by rape or love.

Our youth swirl by,
leaves on a stream,
eddy and turn
at the water's whim,
passing because life passes.

Our aged cling
to life's sheer face
till fingers cramp,
loosen and slip,
then drop to who-knows-where.

Countless faces
yet to be
glare in a dream,
accusing us
of letting them be born

to hack and claw
for a dwindling world,
to thirst and starve,
killing to live,
our Earth dying of man.

Third Symphony in White
after J A M Whistler

How wise, the Japanese,
to place one colour here and there
throughout the whole,
so seeking to please
their Lord of Harmony.   Where
the Eastern soul

stirs into decorative
life it will be filled above all
with deep repose.
Relaxed, dormant, passive,
the two women could almost fall
asleep.   The pose

is delicate, their arms
a fluid line, the fan languidly
dropped from the hand.
Is it that woman's charms
need the submissive touch? And did he
understand?

Nobody's

How absolute a love
that I, on impulse, say,
apropos nothing, 'Stay
near to me always'! Move

elsewhere, we'd surely meet
again, still wondering if
two others suffer grief
to make our love complete.

Does our love, innocent,
plunder theirs empty? Whose
vast scales, indifferent,
unbalance, win or lose?

Nobody's! Such false guilt
would only dare to rise
where harvest ricks stand built
and love's abundance lies.

Another Morning
after Jules Supervielle

A courtyard full of cagebird song;
a housemaid, ironing, recalls sin
with faithless lovers (was it wrong?);
my soul takes it all in.

As milk is clanked upstairs at dawn,
I seem to hear her lovers' speech,
scornful, disparaging, forlorn;
these sounds call each to each,

daybreak's sad chorus. And our bones
must age — mere thirty years become
forty. In the distance moans
the long roll of death's drum.

Tchaikovski's Mistress

I prefer to think of you from afar and to hear you
speak in your music and share your feelings through it.
                              Nadejda von Meck

That was the best way;
to fortify his art
held by her rouble sway
insistent miles apart

and to forbid his hand,
his lips or ardent gaze
materially form
the passion art conveys;

by this possess such love
that no flesh could disgrace
and unmolested feel
his celibate embrace

after his hands were dust,
by time left unbetrayed,
still to her wasting breast
clasp what he made.

Gwen John
(1876-1939)

When love blew out its lamp
she took long solitary walks
wearing fireflies in her hair.
She dreamed herself as a
tall deep-rooted blossom
too singular for cutting
and cultivated passion
in a small inner garden,
growing anonymity like a flower.

Naked with Rodin,
she was still the child
who, casting off her clothes,
went running wild
along the Pembroke beaches.
Scorned, her passion
blossomed through her pain;
years of her letters
drifted on him like petals.

Life was a flowering briar,
its petals falling,
leaving only thorns.
Her God said clasp them
and so inch her way
nearer a better country.
People were only shadows
and she too a shadow,
her body's patient executioner.

Her Dieppe grave's unknown;
if you find it
mark it with her name:
'God's Little Artist'.

At the Auschwitz Factory
after Primo Levi

Gray daybreak again,
a line of torn feet
on the damned earth.
Smoke drags itself from the chimneys,
vicious whistles cut the morning to shreds
and the crowd of dead faces
inherits the suffering day.

You are in my heart, tired friend,
your eyes betray the nothing,
the cold hunger in your breast.
The remnant of courage
within you is broken;
you have no colour.
Once you were strong,
a woman walked beside you;
now you are empty and have no name.
You are forsaken and cannot weep,
your poverty is without grieving,
your weariness without fear.

Broken, once-strong man,
if we were to meet again
under the world's benevolent sun,
how could we face each other?

The Poet to His Soul
after Juan Ramón Jiménez

Day after day you keep the branch protected
in case the rose may come; your ear stays
receptive at your body's gate; always
you go alert for the arrow unexpected.

Nothing can flow from the endless vacancy
out there, and into us, except through your
antenna.   On the universe's door
you are a lock eager to take life's key.

You stamp your seal on all things which then turns
into a universal dynamo
that resurrects on all your seal encloses.
Your rose has been the pattern of all roses,
your ear all harmony, your light all glow,
your fire shining in every star that burns.